CCSS Genre Realistic Fiction

Essential Question
What sounds can you hear? How are they made?

W9-BYD-563

Going on a
Bird Walk

by Amy Helfer

illustrated by Mike Reid

Chapter 1
Dee Gets a Surprise. 2

Chapter 2
It Takes a Little Practice 6

Chapter 3
A Day with the Birds 8

Respond to Reading 12

PAIRED READ How to Make a Wind Chime. . 13

STEM Focus on Science. 16

Chapter 1
Dee Gets a Surprise

"Dee! A package came for you in the mail!" Mom yelled. "It's from Grammy!"

Dee scrambled downstairs to see what her grandmother sent. It wasn't even close to her birthday. She didn't know what to expect.

"What is it?" Dee asked her mother.

"I don't know," her mother answered. "But the only way to find out is to open it!"

Dee ripped through the brown paper and opened the box.

She took out something strange. It was a small wooden spool attached to a metal key. Then she took out a book with pictures of colorful birds on the cover. The title of the book was *Common Birds and Their Calls.*

"Oh, look!" Dee said. "There's a CD, too! And here's a note from Grammy."

Dee opened the note. It said:

Dear Dee,
    Grampy and I are going on a bird walk in two weeks. We would love to take you with us!

    Read the book and listen to the CD. Then practice using the bird call to make bird sounds. See you soon!
Love,
Grammy

"This must be the bird call," Dee said. "Is this how you use it?"

Dee held the wooden part of the bird call in one hand. She held the metal key in the other. Then she twisted the key.

Chapter 2
It Takes a Little Practice

SCREEE!

"Ouch! That hurts my ears!" Dee said. "Let me try this instead."

She twisted the bird call again.

SCREEE-screee!

"It takes practice," laughed Mom. "You'll get it if you keep trying."

Dee read and listened and practiced. She made screeches and squeaks. She made tweets and chirps. She really didn't think the bird call would work.

Early one morning, Grammy and Grampy came to pick up Dee. They drove to a beautiful park for a bird walk.

Chapter 3
A Day with the Birds

Dee and her grandparents walked down a path and into the woods.

Suddenly, Grampy said, "What was that?"

Dee listened, but she heard nothing.

"There it is again," said Grampy.

"Oh!" Dee said quietly. "That sounds like a chickadee!"

Grammy put her arm around Dee.

"You're right!" Grammy said proudly.

Dee took the bird call from her pocket. She twisted the key just as she had practiced.

"Your bird call made him come!" called Grammy. "Look!"

Dee looked where Grammy pointed. There was the same bird that was in her book!

"Wow!" she said. "I never thought this thing would work, but it does!"

"Good job," said Grampy. "Now let's see what else we can find."

Dee heard many birds that day. She knew what most of them were before she even saw them.

"I never knew that so many birds lived near my house," she said. "Each bird sounds so different from the others. Each bird has its own color, too!"

Dee felt so happy on the drive home. "I can't wait to go on a bird walk again," she thought.

"Until then," she thought, "I'll draw pictures of all the birds I saw today. And I'll keep practicing bird sounds with my bird call!"

Respond to Reading

Retell

Use your own words to retell *Going on a Bird Walk.*

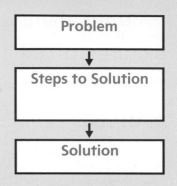

Text Evidence

1. Look at page 6. What problem does Dee have? Problem and Solution

2. Look at page 9. Did Dee solve her problem? How do you know? Problem and Solution

3. How do you know that *Going on a Bird Walk* is realistic fiction? Genre

Compare Texts
Read how to make a wind chime.

Purestock/Getty Images

How to Make a Wind Chime

Follow the steps to make your own wind chime.

Step 1 Have an adult punch four holes around the edge of a paper cup. Poke another hole through the middle of the bottom of the cup. Cut 5 pieces of string or yarn. They should each be about 12 inches long.

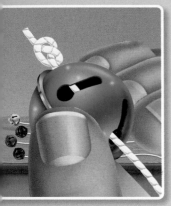

Step 2 Tie a jingle bell to one end of each yarn piece. Tie a good knot.

Step 3 Cut drinking straws into pieces. String straws and wooden beads on the pieces of yarn. Leave some room at the top.

Illustration: Rob Schuster

Step 4 Tie four pieces of yarn through the four holes around the cup edge. Make knots.

Step 5 Take half a pipe cleaner. Bend one end into a loop. Tie and knot the last piece of yarn through the loop. Push the straight end of the pipe cleaner all the way through the last hole.

Step 6 Make another loop at the top of the pipe cleaner. Hang your wind chime outdoors.

Make Connections

Birds and wind chimes are two sounds you can hear outside. What other sounds do you hear? Text to Self

Focus on
Science

Purpose To sort the sounds that you hear around you

What to Do

Step 1 ▶ Think about the sounds you hear during the day and at night.

Step 2 ▶ Make a chart like this one.

Daytime Sounds	Nighttime Sounds

Step 3 ▶ Write three daytime sounds and three nighttime sounds.

Conclusion Which sound was loudest? Which sound was softest? Which sound was your favorite?